BRUCE SPRINGSTEEN
Nancy Robison

Modern Publishing
A Division of Unisystems, Inc.
New York, New York 10022

Printed in Canada

Cover Photo:
The Associated Press

Cover Design: John J. Zboyan/MARKER II STUDIO
Book Design: Judith Teener Graphic Design

Copyright ©1985 Modern Publishing
A Division of Unisystems, Inc.
All Rights Reserved

Book Number: 22580
ISBN Number: 0-87449-049-9

CONTENTS

When Bruce plays his guitar, the crowd roars in appreciation. Tom Herde

INTRODUCTION

His fans chant, "Brr-uu-ce! "Brr-uu-ce!" They hold up lighted matches, stomp their feet on the floor, shout, cheer and roar for, "Brr-uu-ce!" to come on stage. When he finally appears, the crowd goes into a frenzy. Then they settle down to hear the words sung and written by Bruce Springsteen.

A man of the people, Bruce Springsteen leaps into the audience while singing "Tenth Avenue Freeze-out." He races up stairs to play to his fans in the back of the auditorium. Occasionally he brings someone on stage to dance with him, or he might even pick out an interesting face from the crowd and sing to it all night. He's everywhere—on top of speakers, sliding across the stage on his knees, and hopping backwards around the microphone. For four hours each show, Bruce sings, plays and dances his heart out. He can hush a crowd while playing his harmonica, or bring them to their feet, screaming, when he beats his guitar. He's a star who interacts with his fans, and they love it!

In this era of punk rockers with creative hairstyles and crazy outfits, Bruce Springsteen can be himself. At times he wears a stubble of beard on his chin, but his hair is not dyed, gelled or shaved. Neither he nor his band members have to shock the audience to please them, they just have to sing and play their incredible music.

Comfortable with his audience, Bruce often sits on the edge of the stage, legs hanging over into the pit, and tells stories. "I almost became a baseball player," he says with a smile. "That is before rock 'n' roll saved me!" The crowd is easily drawn in by his words and mesmerized by his antics.

"When I was a child," he says, "I was shy, small and skinny. I never belonged or fit in anywhere. I felt like I was on the outside looking in...you know?"

His audience *is* with him. They cheer. They know what he's talking about. Many have felt the same way.

A real showman, Bruce dons a huge cowboy hat to sing "Sherry Darling" or flings his guitar to Clarence Clemons, his saxophone player, and does a few dance steps until his shirt is soaking wet. Sometimes Bruce and Clarence will clown around together. Starting at opposite ends of the stage, they charge each other, as if they were in a bull ring. Both on stage and off Bruce has fun.

Bruce Springsteen truly loves his work. Nils Lofgren a guitarist with the E Street Band says, "With Bruce it's as if someone said, 'You've got four hours left on earth. What are you going to do with it?'"

That's an easy question for Bruce to answer. For Bruce Springsteen, playing rock and roll is first, last and always. Now, is what matters. Not yesterday. Not tomorrow.

The beat goes on and after a four hour show, of singing, dancing, and screaming, Bruce is exhausted, but happy. And so are his fans. They leave the concert hall in the early morning hours smiling and feeling good for having been a part of Bruce Springsteen's life.

"The Boss" as he looked in his high school yearbook photo.
Newsweek Magazine

STARTING OUT

Born in 1949, in Freehold, New Jersey, Bruce Springsteen was the oldest of three children. His mother, Adele, worked as a secretary during most of his childhood. Douglas Springsteen, his father, was a bus driver and often out of work. Bruce and his father never had much to say to each other. For a while Bruce didn't feel as if he fit in anywhere. He thought of himself as being different from the kids at school. Probably because he preferred to be alone and think. He had a creative mind, but hadn't really begun to channel his creative energies.

During those years, Bruce felt small, lonely, weak and helpless. And later, he said about his childhood, "When you're young, you feel powerless. If you're a child you're looking up at everything in the world. The world is frightening. Your house, no matter how small it is, seems so big. Your parents are huge. Your teachers are huge. I don't believe the feeling ever goes away."

Then one day at the ripe old age of thirteen, he noticed a bright yellow guitar in a pawnshop window—and his life changed. Even though he'd never had a music lesson he had to have that guitar. He knew he could learn to play the instrument on his own and somehow he knew being a guitarist would make a big difference in his life.

"It was the most beautiful sight I'd ever seen in my life," he said.

Fortunately, Bruce's cousin could play the guitar a little. Bruce bought the instrument for $18.00, and then his cousin showed him how to play a few chords. That was all Bruce needed. Playing and practicing took up all of his time. While others his age were talking about girls and cars, Bruce was concentrating only on music. With the guitar in his arms he felt a little stronger. There was power in the instrument when he played it! He could feel it!

Listening and studying the records of Elvis Presley, Buddy Holly, Chuck Berry, Bob Dylan and other favorites, Bruce began to imitate them. But it wasn't as easy as he thought. He didn't know how to tune his guitar to make it sound like those played by the other rock and rollers. So, he decided to write his own material to fit his own sound. Much to his amazement the songs poured out of him. He'd write as many as ten a week. And most of them weren't bad.

One day, while watching himself practice in the mirror, he smiled at the image that peered back. It was that of a nice looking boy with a split between his front teeth, brown hair that was neatly combed and just touching the forehead, swept across to one side. It was a plain ordinary looking Dutch-Italian school boy's face. It was then he decided he needed a look...a new image to make him stand out a little. So he tied a bandanna around his forehead, put another one around his neck, ripped the sleeves out of a T-shirt and put on an old pair of faded jeans. Soon the image appeared. What he now saw in the mirror was a rock and roll star just like Elvis Presley. Well, maybe not. He was only Bruce Springsteen—a nobody—a kid with a dream. Rock stars had to work hard to get where they were. He wasn't afraid of hard work. Maybe, just maybe, the dream *could* come true. Time was on his side. Within seconds, he made a decision. He would devote his life to music. It was, afterall, the only thing that mattered in the whole world!

From then on Bruce played and practiced. He worked hard to learn all the chords and to play them fast and without looking. Callouses formed on his fingers. His wrists and arms ached from the new strumming exercises he did. He was devoted to learning the instrument and the results soon appeared.

The sound was getting better. Confidence in himself was growing. It was growing so much, that he wasn't afraid to play in front of others. Soon he gathered some new friends who played guitars and other instruments. They got together and formed a small band. They called themselves the CASTILES. Among this group was "Miami" Steve Van Zandt, a guitarist; Clarence Clemons, a saxophone player; Garry Tallent, who played bass; and a drummer named Bart Hanes.

They had great fun making sounds and pretending they were better than they were. And of course, the dream of becoming famous was always there. They recorded their first and only record, "That's What You Get" and "Baby I." But it was never released. Bruce was only sixteen. He was a young man walking a long hard road. He knew there was still time. Someday all the pieces would fit together and when that day would come he'd be ready.

Bruce and his friend, "Miami" Steve Van

Zandt, would often play the money game. "What will we do if we ever make it?"

"There's big bucks in recordings. Do you think we'll ever make a lot?"

Bruce's family didn't understand his dream. They wanted him to finish school. Bruce tried. After graduating from Freehold High School, he enrolled in Ocean County College. He gave it a try, but he was more interested in music and dropped out to play rock and roll with his friends in a New Jersey club.

Then the Vietnam war came along. Some of Bruce's friends were leaving to join up. Others were getting drafted. Students in school were exempt from the draft. Since Bruce was no longer in school, he was likely to be called upon by the draft.

One day, Bart Hanes, the drummer in the band said, "I joined the Marines."

Bart was always joking around, so Bruce didn't believe him. But this time, Bart was serious. "Well, I've enlisted," he said. "I'm going to Vietnam, wherever that is!"

He left. And he never came back. Undoubtedly, the memory of Bart stayed with Bruce, and later in his career when he wrote songs about the veterans of Vietnam, he may have been thinking of his friend, Bart Hanes.

When Bruce and some band members

were called by the draft, Bruce was only nineteen. Like so many young men, he really didn't want to go to war. His father had been in World War II and believed the discipline of army life would be good for his son. But when Bruce took his physical, he was given a 4–F rating, which means he didn't pass, due to a head injury from a motorcycle accident two years before.

So it was back to the club on the Jersey shore. And while there, he proved himself to be the fastest guitarist around. Everyone called him "The Boss" and the name stuck.

GREETINGS FROM ASBURY PARK, NEW JERSEY

When Bruce was twenty, his family moved to California. Bruce didn't go. He stayed behind and lived in a surfboard factory operated by Carl "Tinker" West. On weekends, Bruce would take a bus into downtown Manhattan . He'd look up at the tall buildings. Music was in this city, and he knew he wanted to be part of it.

But how does a new talent break in to the music scene and get listed on the charts? First, he has to have talent. Second, he needs good management. Timing is important but hard work is also necessary. As someone said, "You have to oil the wheels of success and set them in motion." Eager to go forward, to be a part of the rock and roll scene, Bruce got "Tinker" West, the surfboard manufacturer, to be his manager.

West got Bruce a few bookings in small

clubs. Bruce played solo on acoustic-guitar in one of New York City's rock and roll clubs called, Max's Kansas City. It was a popular place where many stars got their start.

Anywhere people would listen, he'd play his music. On some of the gigs he took his band. They played clubs, private parties, firemen's balls, a state mental hospital, Sing Sing prison, trailer parks, rollerdomes, parking lots of shopping areas, even under the screen during the intermission of a drive-in movie. During this time the name of the band changed from the CASTILES to the ROGUES, to the STEEL MILL to DR. ZOOM AND THE SONIC BOOM. Bruce and his friends were young, crazy, ambitious and having fun.

Rock and roll bands were a dime a dozen at this time. And because there were so many, they weren't paid top dollar. Bruce and his group worked for $15 a night. That was all. And they often played from eight at night to five in the morning.

Totally devoted to what they were doing Bruce and the band were persistent. They had a feeling deep down inside that they were good and they would make it.

During the day the band relaxed and played Monopoly. Bruce brought along his own refreshments to the Monopoly tournaments—Pepsi and cupcakes. And because he liked junk food so much, they nicknamed him "the Gut Bomb King." And when it came time to make a deal, he'd offer one Pepsi for one hotel.

In those days they were living on a dollar a day, seeking work wherever they could find it.

In New York and Philadelphia, rock and roll bands were getting more and more popular. But how many would survive? A group would have to be very good to last.

The Boss kept writing songs about what he saw happening around him, and he wrote with spirit. But nothing big was going on.

Then one day, his manager, "Tinker" West, tried to get something rolling. He called Mike Appel, who had written a television show or two and asked him if he'd be interested in meeting with Bruce, and perhaps becoming his manager. Appel agreed to meet The Boss and asked him to bring along some songs he'd written. Bruce hopped on the bus and while riding, wrote more songs. Appel was impressed, but didn't sign Bruce up right away. He asked him to go home and write some more. Bruce did. Finally in March 1972, Mike Appel said he'd take Bruce on. Bruce hastily signed contracts with Appel without reading them carefully. He didn't know he was signing away his publicity and recording rights. He believed in Mike Appel, and hoped Appel believed in him. Appel proved to be energetic. Right away he got busy trying to get Bruce a singing spot at the Superbowl. Andy Williams was already signed to sing "The Star Spangled Banner," and the band Blood, Sweat and Tears was going to be the halftime entertainment. So Bruce was going to perform with heavyweights of the music world.

Mike Appel got Bruce in to see John Hammond at Columbia Records, who had signed on Billie Holiday, Aretha Franklin and Bob Dylan. After much talking on the part of Mike Appel, Bruce finally got to play his music. Hammond was surprised. He told *Newsweek* magazine, "The kid absolutely knocked me out. I only hear someone really good once every ten years and not only was Bruce the best, he was a lot better than Bob Dylan when I first heard *him*."

Bruce was signed with Columbia Records as a singer-songwriter, and *Greetings from Asbury Park, New Jersey*, was the title of his first album, which he and Mike Appel produced. It came out in January 1973. At this time, the E Street Band was not yet formed. Bruce sang with an acoustic-guitar and a band that included Vinnie Lopez on drums, Clarence Clemons on sax, Gary Tallent on bass, David Sancious on piano and organ.

Their sound was augmented by pianist Harold Wheeler and bassist Richard Davis.

Bruce's songs were original and catchy. Because of his street poetry, he was promoted as the "new Dylan." But that wasn't enough. The records had to be played to be heard, and heard to be bought. What they needed was air time.

Columbia Records began the push. They sent out records to disc jockeys starting with a pop station in New York. But the recordings were set aside and never played. Columbia sent records to other stations around the country too, but with the same results. No one played Bruce Springsteen's records. Without air time, no one could hear the music, and without hearing it first, no one would buy the records. So what happened? Bruce Springsteen's first album died. Although it eventually sold 50,000 copies. Even though a few stations picked up on the music and played the records and Bruce got good reviews in some of the rock magazines, it wasn't enough. The public had to see Bruce Springsteen in action. They had to put a face together with the sound. Bruce knew he'd have to go on the road—to tour. So he got his friends together and formed the E Street Band. In the summer of 1973, Bruce made his first public appearance, other than the small clubs he'd been

"The Boss" and the E Street Band. Charlyn Zlotnik

playing. But it didn't go over very well. The fans weren't responding. Even though, he played on and on, singing his heart out, yet knowing the timing just wasn't right.

Mike Appel kept on promoting Bruce as the newest thing in rock and roll. He tried to get him before the public. Warm-up acts, or opening acts, was all Appel could get for the band. That meant a short forty-five minute show: a second billing. Bruce didn't like that. He played behind the opening act for the up and coming group, Chicago. But he wanted to be the main attraction: the headliner. If only people could see him work. Forty-five minutes was barely a warm-up for his own band. He needed a real chance.

In November 1973, Bruce and the E Street Band cut a second album called, *The Wild , the Innocent and the E Street Shuffle.* It received great reviews in rock magazines and was called one of the best albums of the year. But it didn't sell very well because again the disc jockeys were not playing it. Columbia Records considered dropping him. So Bruce decided to take his music to the people. To let the public hear the music live. Bruce and the E Street Band went on the road. They played true rock classics plus some original music. For two years they criss-crossed the United States playing in towns like Austin, Philadelphia, New York, Phoenix and Cleveland. Finally Bruce was gaining a grassroots following.

It was hard work. The band and Bruce were only making $50 a week. And most of that was used on transportation, food and lodging. A little bit was spent on relaxation— playing pinball.

Hard work and perseverance began to pay off. Bruce began singing songs about average people and their problems. He was called the "Blue Collar Troubadour." More and more, requests came through for his recordings. Bruce was becoming a success.

Then an editor for *Rolling Stone* magazine heard Bruce play in Boston's Harvard Square Theatre. He was impressed with what he heard and wrote, "I saw rock and roll future, and its name is Bruce Springsteen." The editor's name was Jon Landau and his article was the turning point in Bruce's career.

For many years, Bruce had been working on his style and fine tuning his talent. He'd learned to play just about everything and now at last, he was being noticed. The inner desire to keep going, was still there. His third album was recorded. This was his third and maybe his last chance to really succeed. It had to be good.

Danny Federici was on the organ and

Bruce Springsteen and friends. Charlyn Zlotnik

Mighty Max Weinberg on drums, with "Miami" Steve Van Zandt on guitar and Clarence Clemons on sax, how could they miss?

But there was a problem. The songs were not coming out right. Bruce heard something in his head but it wasn't what was coming out on the record. After nine months, try as he did, the music and lyrics were still not right.

Nonetheless, Mike Appel, sent preview records out to the radio stations. The disc jockeys wanted to hear more. Bruce worked for six months trying to get it just right. Yet he was still having trouble getting the sound he wanted onto the record.

Then Jon Landau quit his job at the magazine and became a promoter for Bruce Springsteen records in 1975. He got Columbia Records to promote the first two Springsteen albums. They did so, adding that a third album was on the way. Now Bruce *had* to get it finished. The first two albums sold more than they had the first time out. Both eventually earned gold record awards.

There is a saying, "If you keep shaking the tree, the leaves are bound to fall." And Bruce kept shaking until the music came.

Jon Landau said about him, "Bruce works instinctively. He is incredibly intense, and he concentrates deeply. Underneath his shyness is the strongest will I've ever encountered. If

The Born to Run *album becomes gold—1975.* Peter Greenberg/Newsweek Magazine

there's something he doesn't want to do, he won't."

Bruce worked from three in the afternoon until six in the morning and sometimes around the clock without stopping. And that was it. They had the perfect rock sound. The album was finished. It was called *Born to Run!*

By this time, Bruce Springsteen had quite a following and when tickets went on sale for a performance in Greenwich Village, the tickets sold out in three days. Columbia Records was so sure of Bruce's talent that they bought a third of the tickets and sent them to nearby disc jockeys who had been playing his music. They told them to go see the show and if they liked it to play his records. If not, they weren't obligated to play Bruce's music.

One of those present was the disc jockey who had refused to play Bruce's first album. But after seeing him in person, he changed his mind. The next day he made an apology on the air by saying, "I saw Springsteen for the first time last night. It's the most exciting rock and roll show I've ever seen."

Sales on his third album, *Born to Run*, began to roll in. In a matter of months, it zoomed to number three on the charts, selling over 600,000 copies making it a gold record. Ultimately, *Born to Run* would sell over one million copies and turn platinum! A lot better than his first album which only sold 50,000 copies.

The record company earned millions of dollars. Plus the sales gave Bruce a little more money in his pocket. But Bruce didn't really care about the money. There wasn't much he wanted to buy, except for a fancy 1957 yellow Chevy convertible with orange flames painted along the sides. He'd often admired the car. It reminded him of his first guitar.

He also rented a small cottage near Asbury Park, and the rest of the money he used to pay off old debts. With twenty-two people on his payroll, plus expensive lighting and sound equipment, the money went fast. And even though he was now well on his way to super stardom, Bruce added only one thing to his costume: a small gold ring in his right ear!

Souvenirs from the Born to Run Tour—Springsteen takes America by storm! Robert R. McElroy/Newsweek

BORN TO RUN

In September 1975, National Educational Television (NET) in Chicago taped a show on John Hammond of Columbia Records. The show introduced some of the talent he'd signed. Bob Dylan and Aretha Franklin were among the guests, and so was BRUCE SPRINGSTEEN. He had reached celebrity status!

After the album *Born to Run* was launched, Springsteen's name and picture appeared everywhere. On October 27, 1975 both *Time* and *Newsweek* put his picture on the covers of their magazines in the same week. And his first commercial recording became a smash hit. Bruce Springsteen had made it. He was the newest rock hero. He hit super stardom.

"*Born to Run*," he says, "really deals with faith and a searching for answers. On that record I laid out a set of values. A set of ideas—intangibles like faith and hope, belief in friendship and in a better day. But you don't really know what those values are worth until you test them."

Of course with publicity came questions. People wondered if Bruce could hold up under all the talk and publicity and if too much happened to him too soon.

Some said he was, "Only a twenty-year-old kid with a beard." Others called the publicity "hype" meaning he didn't have any talent, it was all just talk.

Mike Appel, his manager answered the questions by saying, "What we're all waiting for is something that makes us want to dance. And Springsteen's got it. Wake up America!"

Bruce's answer was a little more humble. "If the music is right, I will survive. But if the music goes wrong, then that is the end of it."

Well, his music did survive and it looked as if *Born to Run* should be re-titled, BORN TO SUCCEED! With his picture and write-ups on him appearing in leading magazines, it looked as if Bruce was a genuine rocker.

His new fame took him to London. He'd never been there before and didn't know what to expect. Seeing a poster that said, "Finally, the world is ready for Bruce Springsteen." he tore it down. The pressures of

Bruce Springsteen and Clarence Clemons rock out! Bernard Gotfryd/Newsweek

Bruce strikes a familiar pose during his Born to Run Tour–1975. Bernard Gotfryd/Newsweek

stardom were beginning to get to him. Fame and attention are hard to take all in one swallow, and Bruce wasn't ready to gulp it down.

When it came time to perform, Bruce bombed. Perhaps he had a sudden case of stage fright, or thought he couldn't live up to his publicity. Whatever it was, it showed. The audience was disappointed at his performance. So was Bruce. He knew he could do better. Five nights later, in the same auditorium, he had another chance. This time he gave a snappy, sharp show earning back his self-respect.

But then a crisis appeared in his career. The Boss found it necessary to sue his manager Mike Appel in Manhattan's U.S. District Court for fraud and breach of trust. Appel counter-sued in New York's Supreme Court over recording and publicity rights. For nearly two years, Bruce's rock and roll career was complicated by a lawsuit and he was not permitted to record. But during this time, he kept writing and other artists performed his songs.

In 1978, Manfred Mann recorded Bruce Springsteen's "Blinded by the Light," and he received his first gold record. On the flip side was another Springsteen song, "Spirit In the Night."

Bruce mesmerizes the Atlanta, Georgia audience during his Born to Run Tour—1975. Ron Sherman

In 1979, the Pointer Sisters recorded Bruce's "Fire," and got a gold record for it.

Bruce Springsteen's music was even a hit in the ballet circuit. Twyla Tharp, a choreographer, included a Springsteen number in one of her shorter dances.

While waiting for the lawsuit to be over, Bruce had time to think of what he really wanted. He'd had a little taste of success, was he willing to sacrifice friends to attain the ultimate? He began to understand just how important music and his friends were.

"Music keeps me alive," he said. "And my relationships with friends—that's my life-blood. And to give that up for cars, houses and stuff, that's not the American dream. That's the booby prize, in the end. And if you fall for them—if when you achieve them, you believe that this is the end in itself, then you've been suckered in. Because those are the consolation prizes if you're not careful, for selling yourself out, or letting the best of yourself slip away. You've got to carry the idea you began with further. And you've got to hope that you're headed for higher ground."

The time it took to reach a settlement also offered The Boss and the E Street Band a chance to practice and refine their sound.

Finally, when the lawsuit was settled—out of court—Bruce got the rights back to his

Springsteen and Clemons have a rousing duet. Charlyn Zlotnik

songs and the privilege to choose his own producer. And Columbia Records signed him on again. For these privileges, Bruce had to pay his ex-manager, Mike Appel, nearly one million dollars.

But it was worth it in the long run. From then on, Bruce was free to make his own contracts. And you can be sure he now reads the small print. Almost immediately, his friend and promotor, Jon Landau stepped in as his new manager and he has been with The Boss ever since.

So, Bruce weathered the storm. He kept writing and singing about real people with real problems. The public recognized his tal-

"The Boss" is seen strolling along a Manhattan street on a cold winter night, 1979. Ron Galella

ent. They listened to his messages. He was singing to them—about them.

In 1978, Bruce Springsteen's album, *Darkness on the Edge of Town* was released. It was about a lonesome guy in the real world, who can't handle his loneliness. Not all the reviews were good. Some said the lyrics were full of "breast-beating" and "woe-is-me" type lyrics. Nevertheless, the album climbed to the number five position on the charts.

Along with Patti Smith, a punk poet, he co-authored, "Because of the Night," in 1978, which reached number thirteen on the charts. It was Patti Smith's only successful record. Bruce played it in concerts.

In 1979, Bruce and the E Street Band appeared in an Anti-Nuclear benefit concert. It was filmed as a documentary entitled, "The MUSE Concert: No Nukes." An anthology LP from the concert was called *No Nukes*. Along with forty rock and roll stars, Bruce signed a petition to President Carter to end nuclear power plants in America. Some of the other performers were, James Taylor, the Doobie Brothers, and Tom Petty and the Heartbreakers.

Then, in 1980, Bruce recorded an album called, *The River.* Reviewers liked it better. It contained songs about other people looking for a way out. Bruce was seeing more clearly outside of himself. He was writing about others.

Some people were saying that Bruce Springsteen was overrated, but The Boss proved them wrong. He hit the road again on a concert tour with the E Street Band and blew the crowds away. Tickets went on sale and sold out almost immediately. Fans thronged to hear the steady beat of rock and roll. For three and a half hours and thirty songs each show, Bruce screamed and sweated under hot lights. The final run of the eleven-month River tour was held at the Riverfront Coliseum in Ohio, in 1981. It was the first concert held there since the disaster which took place at the 1979 Who concert. But Bruce's promoters assured concert hall officials that The Boss would be able to control the show and they were right. The concert was a success—and safe for both fans and performers.

The Born to Run Tour takes off—Bruce Springsteen at the Roxy, Los Angeles, California—October 16–19, 1975. Peter Greenberg/Newsweek

"HOMECOMING"

Back in 1975, just after Bruce and the band had reached their first breakthrough, they appeared in New Jersey at a movie theater. The word HOMECOMING was put up on the marquee. Everyone knew what it meant. Bruce was back. The same Bruce they'd gone to school with. The same Bruce they'd seen in clubs around New Jersey. Now he was big time. Music critics had written about him and disc jockeys were playing his music. Now he had to prove himself to his hometown crowd. He did. Along with his saxophonist, Clarence Clemons, he put on a show they'd never forget. Ripping away his black leather jacket, and blasting words into the microphone, leaping about the stage and moving as if he were completely at home, Bruce proved what he could do. He was the new rock sensation from New Jersey.

Then Bruce was off to California to make his West Coast debut at the Roxy Night Club on Sunset Strip. Although he may have been nervous about appearing before movie stars, he didn't show it. Here was a rock band for all seasons. A sound that delighted the audience. Bruce Springsteen gave them straight-to-the-heart lyrics. His voice was raspy, but warm. The E Street Band presented a smorgasbord of music from a hint of rockabilly (which was just beginning) to energetic heavy metal. Once again, Bruce gave an electrifying performance and came away a superstar.

The Boss was now called one of the most exciting live acts in rock and roll. Adding to it, Springsteen posters, decals, souvenir buttons, T-shirts, and key chains hit the market.

ABC-TV wanted to do a show on the "Heroes of Rock and Roll." Bruce was asked to be in it. He sang his songs and was compared to rock greats like Elvis Presley, Buddy Holly, the Beatles, Bob Dylan, Chuck Berry. The film was narrated by Jeff Bridges and was quite a success.

By now Bruce and the E Street Band had made quite a name for themselves as a dynamic energetic act. Asked where he got the energy to perform for three and a half hours a night, three nights in a row, Bruce answered, "I've got a lot of energy. It just comes naturally.

But when I get on stage and I'm running on empty, I just think of the promise that's made from hundreds or thousands of miles away. Some guy has bought this ticket and there's a promise made between musician and the audience. When they support each other, that's a special thing. It's no different than if you stood with this person and shook his hand."

Bruce also says that the audience has a lot to do with inspiring the performer on. Even when the performer is exhausted with nothing left to give, the audience can revitalize him or her with its enthusiasm.

Bruce also says, "What you do tonight, you don't make up for tomorrow, and you don't ride on what you did last night. Tonight is tonight. I always keep in mind that you have only one chance." This is what he believes and he doesn't take it lightly.

That doesn't mean that Bruce never gets tired. To say that would be ridiculous. After the show each night, he goes to his dressing room backstage, and soaks himself in liniment. And he drinks a glass of mineral water —nothing stronger.

"If you smell something weird," he might say and he'll laugh when he adds, "That's me! I put that stuff all over me, because otherwise in three or four hours, I become very similar to a table."

You would think that anyone leaping in the air, jumping up and down and screaming at the top of his lungs, would become stiff, but Bruce doesn't think that's why. He believes the soreness comes from just breathing. He says, "The whole top of your body goes in and out for hours. Try it yourself for just twenty minutes and see how you feel." Undoubtedly, Bruce puts his all into every show. And there's no denying his fans appreciate it!

A CHARITABLE MAN

Bruce kicked off his 1980–81 tour by playing in the Brendan Byrne Arena in New Jersey. It was brand new and The Boss and the E Street Band were the first to play there. They were there six nights and played to 20,000 fans each night. That's 120,000 people.

The arena was built with rock and roll concerts in mind. Sound panels and insulation were everywhere in the building, which reduced the echoing and bouncing effect, which happens at indoor concerts. Speakers with high quality sound were placed right above the stage. And it was great. Bruce said about this engagement, "That was the best show ever. We couldn't hear each other on stage. I felt like the Beatles."

Tickets to his concerts were selling out fast. Although Bruce preferred playing to smaller audiences, the only way to meet ticket demands was to play in large arenas. So he met the demand and played in places usually reserved for pro sports events.

The 1980–81 tour included new songs like "The River" and "Wreck on the Highway." They played 122 shows on the tour. The band played clearly. Their sound was lighter and crisper than it ever had been. They played hard every single night in every town. People began to take notice and passed the word along. "You've just got to see this show!" was commonly heard.

Money was pouring into Springsteen's bank account. With records selling in the millions you could say, The Boss was getting rich. Although money was part of his early dream, he never played or did a show for money. He always tries to keep his concert ticket prices low, around $15 a seat. But scalpers—those who buy the tickets and then resell them for more—take advantage of the low price. At a recent concert, front row seats sold for $2500 each!

Bruce speaks of money in this way, "I think if I did play just for the money, people would know, and they'd throw me out. And I'd deserve it."

An interview with *Rolling Stone* magazine asked Bruce, "Obviously you don't spend your money on clothes, what do you do with it?"

The Boss answered, "Having money lets you do the things you want to do. For one thing, you don't have to worry about rent. You can buy things for your folks and help out your friends. And you can have a good time. I don't know if money changes you. It's a convenience."

Throughout his career, Bruce has put his money to good use. He's helped out friends that were down on their luck—Gary U.S. Bonds for one. Not only did Bruce loan him money, but he recorded a couple of songs with him to help him back on his feet. In return, when Gary U.S. Bonds recovered, he gave Bruce a 1969 Chevy for his car collection.

Bruce also participated in a Peace Walk rally that was held in New York's Central Park in June 1982. The rally featured other stars includng James Taylor, Linda Ronstadt and Joan Baez.

In 1979, he appeared in a five night concert for Musicians United for Safe Energy (MUSE) in Madison Square Garden, New York, as one of his benefit engagements.

Bruce even asked his manager Jon Landau, to find out how he could help the Vietnam veterans. Jon Landau learned that the Veterans Administration would be delighted to have Bruce do a benefit show in their honor. They needed help and accepted his offer. So, in 1981, Bruce performed for three nights at a concert held at the Los Angeles Sports Arena. This sold-out show earned about $100,000. Also, a Bruce Springsteen poster was made and sold with all the monies going to the Vietnam Veterans of America (VVA) fund. Before the concert, Bruce introduced a veteran who after a few words thanked Bruce Springsteen and the other artists for sharing their time in a benefit performance for the VVA. Then he introduced The Boss who took the stage and led the E Street Band in several rollicking numbers.

When asked how he felt about doing these benefits, Bruce told reporters, "It's like when you're walking down a dark street at night and out of the corner of your eye, you see somebody getting hurt in a dark alley, but you keep walking on because you think it doesn't have anything to do with you. You just want to get home. Vietnam turned the whole country into that dark street, and unless we can walk down those dark alleys and look into the eyes of those men and women, we're never going to get home."

Even at his regular shows, Bruce dedicates songs to those in need including the United Steel Workers and various environmental organizations. And he makes re-marks to the audience to look into the groups and see if they can help.

He has donated checks for as much as $10,000 of his own money, to local food banks. And he has made pleas for others to do the same. "Give what you can," he suggests. But this is as far as his politics go.

After over a year on the road, The Boss and the E Street Band took a rest. Bruce said 1980–81 had been the best year of his life. They had played to over one million people and traveled across America and parts of Europe.

On the last night of the last show, two stage crew members dressed up as police officers. They hung out at both ends of the stage. Then they pretended to close the show, telling Bruce he was running overtime. They ran on to the stage, grabbed The Boss and carried him away. But Bruce broke away from them and got back to the front of the stage without missing a single beat. The audience loved it and wanted more.

Afterward, an end-of-the-tour celebra-tion lasted until dawn. Then The Boss was off to take a well-deserved rest.

Springsteen and the E Street Band, including Nils Lofgren, gave an unannounced concert at the Stone Pony in Asbury Park, New Jersey, 1984. James Shive/Retna Ltd.

THE PRICE OF FAME

After twelve years of hard work, Bruce finally bought something for himself—a mansion on the hill in Rumson, New Jersey. "It's the kind of place I told myself I'd never live in," he said. Until then he had been renting a small house in New Jersey.

His new home has a swimming pool and garages which hold his car collection consisting of a pick-up truck, a Chevy convertible, a Corvette and a Camaro. Before he got his home, he stashed his cars in friends' garages.

With a home comes roots. Bruce never felt as if he wanted to be rooted. That's where his hit album title came from—*Born to Run*.

Driving alone in his car, feeling loose and the freedom to go anywhere, anytime is what he wanted. "Someday, maybe, I'd like to have the whole nine yards—a wife and kids," he'd said, "but not yet."

Around this time, he wrote, "I Wanna Marry You," so maybe he *was* thinking about the whole nine yards more than he was willing to admit.

Back then Bruce stayed on the run. His band was his family. When they weren't working, he had his friends over for barbeques and to play softball. For years, he had tried not to be isolated and he wasn't going to start now. Loneliness is painful. Many people before the public eye—Elvis Presley was one—feel as if they have to lock themselves away. They can't live a normal life. They feel a lot of pressure on them wherever they go and can't go anywhere without body guards. And after seeing how confined a life Elvis led, Bruce was even more determined to be a part of the people.

Learning from someone else's lessons is a hard thing to do, but Bruce seems to have learned something from past rock and roll stars. Once he told reporters, "One thing that has shortened the life span, physically and creatively, of some of the best rock and roll musicians is cruel isolation. If the price of fame is that you have to be isolated from people you write for, then that's too high a price to pay." So he still mingles with the public.

Bruce is captured backstage at Spectrum Stadium, Philadelphia, during his sold out 1985 tour. Ron Galella

His friends say, "Bruce tries to control his own life. He's not interested in being an isolated person."

Yet, he does try to keep his private life private. When he's in front of the world, performing, that's different, but there are some things he doesn't talk about.

When The Boss and his E Street Band started out, they may have had dreams of being like Elvis or some rock group. But as they grew up and into their own sound, they began to like themselves for what they were. They were good. They were original. As they became more polished, they became more sure of themselves and their freedom.

In 1982, while Bruce was still renting his house in Colts Neck, New Jersey he concentrated on his writing. For two months he wrote without going out of the house much.

As he wrote, he recorded his songs on a 4-track home cassette machine. He thought that if they sounded good, he'd teach the songs to the band. Alone, he sang and played his guitar, while the machine recorded it. Then with two tracks left, he over-dubbed his guitar. This was to make harmony and to sound like two guitars were playing. It was fun. He mixed through a little echo plex and it sounded pretty good. The tape was only a demo, something he could let the band hear. Then he would show it to the recording company and if they liked it, he'd get the band and they'd record it together.

Without even a case around it, he dropped the cassette into his pocket. It stayed there. Bruce carried it around with him. Days went by. Weeks went by. And doubt set in. It probably wasn't good enough to show anyone, he thought. But when they heard it, in the studio, he realized all that needed to be done, was setting it in wax. He called this collection of songs *Nebraska*. Many of his true fans liked it, but many others didn't. *Nebraska* had a message. He wrote the story and hoped the message got across. It was, he says, "When things get really dark, hold on—don't isolate yourself. Be a part of your community. Take an interest in your job—your town."

Around this same time, Bruce was working on some more songs he liked. And so did the record company. While *Nebraska* was being recorded, they decided to do one side of another new album. Bruce called it, *Born in the USA!*

"I was born in the U.S.A!"—Springsteen in concert, Phila-delphia 1985. Tom Herde

BORN IN THE USA!

Born in the USA, released in 1984, showed Bruce's ability to write blues and ballads, as well as emotional songs and tough rock. People related more with these stories of loneliness, vanishing dreams and a high school hero who didn't succeed than with the type of music he wrote for *Nebraska*.

During the recording sessions, the band played well together. The first song, "Born in the USA" was recorded in one take. The rest of the songs were done in under five takes, which is very quick. Recording doesn't take the time, writing down the words and waiting for inspiration does. Fortunately Bruce is a very inspired songwriter.

The *Born in the USA* album and subsequently the tour of the same name elevated Bruce and the E Street Band to greater heights than they had thought possible. Receiving massive airplay, the album reached number one on *Billboard's* top LPs chart in just three weeks!

Unbelieveably, the band faced many turning points during this time. One of the most important of which was changing band members.

In 1984 Bruce's long time friend and guitarist, "Miami" Steve Van Zandt broke away from the E Street Band to tour with his own group and record his own songs. Nils Lofgren took Steve's place and added some powerful strumming to the group. For a month before the 1984–85 tour, Lofgren moved into Bruce's house in Rumson, New Jersey and learned the songs. He had met Bruce in the 1960's when they auditioned together for a club act. Over the years they kept running into each other, renewing their friendship. So when Steve left, Bruce brought in Lofgren.

Bruce says that Lofgren "fit in naturally and easily. We look at music in the same way, and care about the same things."

Also added to the group in time to rehearse and be part of the year-long tour was singer, Patti Scialfa. "Having a woman up there with us gives it more of a feeling of community," Bruce told reporters.

The 1984–85 E Street Band also features Roy Bittan and Danny Federici who play the keyboards, Garry Tallent on the bass, Max

A romantic duet with band member Patti Scialfa during Bruce's sold-out American tour, 1985. Robin Platzer/ Images

Weinberg on drums, and long time faithful friend, Clarence Clemons on the saxophone.

"The band gets along very well," Roy Bittan says. "We've been together so long it's pretty easy to second guess Bruce. He lets us be creative but gives us sign posts along the way."

The Boss tries to communicate the feeling he's trying to get across. Sometimes it's moody and blue. Sometimes it's full of spark and energy. Sometimes it's just loose. He'll say to the band something like, "We have to play

Singing and dancing to the beat—"The Boss" and Clarence Clemons—Giants Stadium, 1985. Robin Platzer/Images

this sparse and simple. We want a lot of space."

On the 1984–85 tour, Bruce played songs from his *Born in the USA* album. And in general, when in concert, besides playing his own songs, he plays favorites from other bands, like "Street Fighting Man" by the Rolling Stones. And he often pays tribute to Elvis Presley by singing some of his songs.

Even now, during tours or while in concert, Bruce still introduces his songs with personal comments. For *Nebraska* he might say, "This is about being so lonesome you could cry." Or for *Used Cars*, he might say, "If you've ever pushed a car down a street and felt like the biggest jerk in the world, this one's for you." He often shouts at the crowd when he takes off in a fast rock and roll dance, "I ain't shy anymore!" And at the end of the show, he screams, "Let Freedom Ring!"

It's no wonder, then that people respond to his songs. "It's the emotional reality that makes anything real, it's not the details," Bruce said in an interview with reporters about why his songs of loneliness and lowly beginnings touch a chord in just about everybody.

"Maybe it's your imagination or maybe it's some thing out of real life, it doesn't matter. It's the little things that make a song real to

The smile on Springsteen's face says it all. Charlyn Zlotnik

Awesome! Bruce in concert at Giants Stadium, New Jersey, 1985. Larry Busacca/Retna Ltd.

you. Whether it's "My Hometown," "Nebraska" or "Johnny 99," you kind of just got to know what that feels like, somewhere, and everybody does. People respond to it if it's real."

Followers of The Boss call him, "An all-American guy," "A real cool guy," or say "He's for the blue collar worker." His followers are the all-American type people. They actually go to the concerts to hear him sing his songs as well as play the guitar. To see him, they sleep in the streets waiting for concert tickets and line up for hours to get a glimpse of him.

Looking back over The Boss' career, any fan would agree that a rock star who can grab the attention of the public the way Elvis or the Beatles did, is sure to sell a lot of records. And this is just what Bruce Springsteen has done from 1975 to the present time. He has sold millions of records—even after experiencing the various ups and downs of his career. Remarkably, through it all, he never gave up, but kept trying to improve. Hard work was always the key to his success. His voice got huskier and his lyrics got more down to earth. And as the band developed, they kept attracting a wide ranging audience of fans of all ages. The fans' enthusiasm is what really keeps any rocker rolling!

"I WANNA MARRY YOU"

The marriage of Bruce to model-actress, Julianne Phillips, created a lot of publicity. But through it all Bruce has continued to tour, travel and sing his songs—now with Julianne at his side and in the wings to smile at him and cheer him on.

Julianne was born in Chicago, and moved with her family to Oregon when she was seven. In ninth grade she was elected a Christmas Princess and later became a high school cheerleader. She began modeling at a nearby department store as an afternoon afterschool job. This job which paid only minimum wage was a training period for Julianne. Little did she know that someday, as a model in New York, she'd earn as much as $2000 a day.

Like Bruce, Julianne had a lot of ambition and high expectations for herself. Being a model wasn't enough. She wanted to be an actress also. So she moved from New York to California where she was quickly picked up for three television movies.

With Bruce in New Jersey and Julianne in Hollywood, how did they meet? It was when Bruce was playing in concert at the Los Angeles Sports Arena in October 1984. Julianne was there. She saw him and asked to be introduced. Her manager arranged it. They met back stage and that was the beginning. It must have been love at first sight.

They began dating in a peculiar way. He brought her to his health club in New Jersey. And she introduced him to her gym in Beverly Hills, California. They soon became a news item. And when Julianne attended a high school reunion party at Christmas time, her former classmates knew about her new boyfriend, Bruce Springsteen. The news was around and rumors were flying. Would Julianne marry Bruce Springsteen?

Workouts at the health clubs were more fun with Julianne around. Once a junk food addict, Bruce began to eat vegetables, and to put aside the greasy spoon stuff. He began lifting weights and working out in a gym every day and running six miles a day. Another new look in Bruce Springsteen was emerging. But even though he was on a health kick, he had to admit, that he still liked to eat in diners occasionally.

In February while her parents were staying in Palm Springs, California, Julianne decided to introduce Bruce. He was dressed in a tie and suit and made a good impression. He didn't smoke or drink and was very quiet. Could this be the same Bruce Springsteen they'd seen on television. The one who wore cut off rags and jean jackets? Who yelled, gyrated, gritted his teeth and sang in a raspy voice? It couldn't be. But it was the very same Bruce Springsteen who twenty-two years before had looked in the mirror and seen only a shy, skinny nobody. And now that nobody had turned into a handsome, rich and talented man.

A few weeks after the visit to her parents', Julianne attended the Grammy Awards with Bruce. They sat in the front row, waited and hoped that Bruce would get an award. But he lost out to Lionel Richie for Album of the Year. However he couldn't have been too unhappy, for he had Julianne by his side and he wanted to keep her there. So she went along with him on the continuation of his Born in the USA tour. They went to Australia and Japan. On the way back, they stopped in Hawaii where they probably made plans for their secret marriage.

Bruce and his wife, Julianne, share a quiet moment. Paul Simkin/Sygma

Their marriage was a private affair coming in the middle of his 1984–85 tour—a secret from the press and news reporters, but it was also very romantic.

It was a midnight wedding with Bruce wearing a traditional black tuxedo. (Quite a change from leather jacket and jeans.) Julianne wore an off-white lace dress, which she borrowed from a childhood friend. She also wore ankle-length boots and a white waist-length veil.

The wedding took place at Our Lady of the Lake Church in Lake Oswego, near Portland, Oregon, Julianne's hometown. Friends and relatives invited to the midnight affair were sworn to secrecy. Guests arrived three days early, stayed with friends and neighbors and waited for the secret call to the church. Shortly after midnight on May 13th, 1985, that call came in. Guests were picked up and driven to the church, all in secrecy.

Julianne's best friend and her sister were bridal attendants. With Bruce were his long time friends and members of his E Street Band, "Miami" Steve Van Zandt, wearing a black kerchief around his head, saxophonist Clarence Clemons, and manager Jon Landau.

Why all the secrecy? It all started shortly after their engagement. Springsteen had long claimed he was born to run, and he did so and kept running until Julianne caught him —or he caught her. He was considered the most eligible bachelor among the rock stars. Fans, some with broken hearts, and others thrilled with the idea of this handsome couple marrying, flocked to lake Oswego in hopes of seeing the popular couple. The local radio station KKRZ even set up a "Springsteen rumor hotline" for the fans to keep up with the happenings of the couple. They wanted to know where they were and when the wedding was going to take place.

Julianne's home and parents were hounded by reporters. Crowds began to form outside her parents' home. Afraid that their wedding would turn into a circus, Bruce and

Julianne decided to keep the wedding whereabouts a secret.

Bruce put it like this, "I give my entire energy to the public. But this is different. Things that are private should be kept private."

The night of the wedding, when all the reporters were tucked snuggly in for the night, the wedding party sneaked out the back door. They went through neighbors' yards and into a waiting car. At the local high school, they switched cars and quietly got to the church, which had been kept dark so as not to arouse any suspicions.

Shortly after midnight, the couple became, Mr. and Mrs. Bruce Springsteen. They left the church in a round of applause from the guests. Not only because they were newlyweds, but because they had pulled off the marriage ceremony without the press knowing all about it.

When the new Mr. and Mrs. Springsteen were safely away, Julianne's brother phoned KKRZ and gave them the news.

On a combination honeymoon and continuation of the world tour, Mr. and Mrs. Springsteen went to Europe. Bruce appeared in Dublin, Ireland where he showed off the gold ring on his finger. The gold ring in one ear was long gone by now. Sixty-five thousand Irish fans crowded the Slane Castle estate to welcome The Boss and his new bride.

"The Boss" lookin' good!—In concert, Philadelphia—1985.
Tom Herde

"I'M ON FIRE"

With a new set of muscles, a wife and millions of fans, Bruce Springsteen is on fire. And no wonder! Record sales are better than ever, concert tickets are sold out, and his videos, "I'm on Fire" and "Glory Days" are doing well. The Boss always promises a good show and always gives his best. And as the saying goes, "You reap what you sow." Bruce is now receiving the harvest from his crop, that he planted so many years ago. He has watered, fed and taken care of his career and is now enjoying the benefits. He deserves his successes.

As mentioned earlier, Bruce likes to do benefits and will always volunteer his time and talent when called upon. Early in 1985, he was asked to be a part of the, "We Are The World" benefit recording. All proceeds from the sale of the album would go for African relief, to help the starving people in Africa.

In the wee hours of the morning, right after the American Music Awards, Bruce Springsteen and other talented artists gathered at the A & M Recording studios in Los Angeles. Some of the other artists were Cindi Lauper, Michael Jackson, Stevie Wonder, Harry Belafonte and Tina Turner. They had one goal in mind and were willing to spend the early morning hours making this record.

Words and music were written by Michael Jackson and Lionel Richie, but when the other stars arrived, wrinkles in the program arose. Changes needed to be made to suit each particular artist. After a few word changes and a variation in the tune to suit each soloist, the recording session began. They sang as a group and individually.

When it came time for Bruce to sing his solo part, he stepped up to the microphone and asked nervously, as if he'd never performed before, "What do I do?"

Bob Quincy, the director said, "It's just like being a cheerleader of the chorus."

Bruce looked at the sheet music and then stuck it in his back pocket. "I'll give it a shot," he said in a rusty voice.

Dressed in jeans and a leather jacket, he looked a little tired. The night before he had performed in a four hour show in Syracuse and he'd flown most of the day to get to the awards ceremony and the recording session.

The tape rolled. Bruce was given his cue. The unmistakable sound of Bruce Springsteen's scratchy voice bellowed, "We are—we are the children of the world!"

When he'd finished he said into the microphone, "Something like that?"

Bob Quincy laughed, for Bruce had made it right the first time. "*Exactly* like that," he said.

Bruce listened to the playback on his recording. It sounded okay to him and to everyone else. The Boss had scored. It was eight in the morning and time to leave for the next stop on his busy tour. Outside six limousines were lined up to take the stars home. But not one of them was for The Boss. He had rented a car of his own and parked it across the street. He got in it and drove back to the airport.

Several months later there was another show to raise cash for the African famine victims. The show was called, "Live Aid." Many talented artists were present, but Bruce had other commitments and was unable to attend.

In his 1984–85 tour he made a hit in Kyoto, Japan as well as in South Wabash,

Chicago. *Born in the USA* was his seventh album and it was still in the top ten after more than a year. It sold more than 7.5 million copies in America alone and is the biggest seller in the history of Columbia Records. His hand-clapping, dance-till-you-drop tour had a lot to do with promoting sales.

Outside of the United States, the album sold five million copies in twenty countries. On his overseas tour, he visited Britain, West Germany, the Netherlands and more. Bruce was becoming an international symbol of America. Always dressed in blue jeans, T-shirts or shirts with rolled up sleeves, he looked very much like any normal guy you'd meet on the street. There's nothing show-offy about him, which adds to his appeal.

In Australia and Japan, he and the band were well received. In fact one band member commented on it with surprise, "What a response! We felt as if we were in New Jersey!" That's like feeling you're at home.

In Europe kids waved American flags and chanted, "Born in the USA." The *Born in the USA* album was making a strong statement in the world of rock and roll—everywhere in the world. Bruce's songs not only fit America but other countries as well.

In Paris, a radio station said, "The problems of city life and the working class are the same everywhere."

Bruce was a symbol, a hero. European audiences cheered for him wherever he was. His songs were popular because they were full of hope and were easier to relate to.

Friends describe Bruce as humble. "He's not trying to be a hero or an idol or even a symbol of the United States. He's not even trying to get rich. He just wants to play his songs and he cares about those listening to him."

Bruce says, "The types of things that make people's lives heroic are a lot of times very small things. Little things that happen in the kitchen or things between husband and wife or between them and their kids. It's a grand experience but it's not always grandiose. That's what interests me now. There's plenty of room for those types of victories."

Although it's getting harder all the time, loyal friends help Bruce keep his privacy. Bruce is a bigger star than ever. He's become a national symbol—a goodwill ambassador.

His home state, New Jersey is particularly pleased with Bruce's success. A state assemblyman even tried to get Bruce's "Born to Run" named the state song.

In the last few years New Jersey has become a home of "new collar" workers, which is somewhere between white collar

Bruce plays to a sold-out house. Ross Marino/Sygma

"The Boss" takes center stage to belt out a song. Ross Marino/Sygma

and blue collar. Some are saying that Bruce's identity with the working class has had something to do with this change. When he appeared in New Jersey's Meadowlands, in August 1985, a quarter of a million fans showed up. This broke the record he'd only set the week before at Giants Stadium in New Jersey.

The year the album, *Born in the USA* was released, was an election year and some wondered if Bruce was being political. They wondered if he was favoring President Ronald Reagan. Although his songs reflected social concerns, he claimed no such thing. A registered voter, Bruce votes, but won't say who he votes for. That's the American way.

Some think that because the *Born in the USA* album cover has a picture of the American flag that Bruce is into politics and trying to make a statement. But actually he's not. The flag has nothing to do with his feelings or beliefs. Having the American flag on the cover, is impressive, as the American flag always is, and it fit with the title song. That's all.

A musician first, Bruce tries to stay on his own side of the street. If he has a message, he sings about it—broken dreams, lost jobs, shattered families, highway patrolmen, black sheep in the family, working class kid, trapped in a sad marriage, laid off auto worker driven to crime, loneliness, and human needs. Bruce Springsteen is a champ when it comes to singing about matters that all people can relate to.

His 1984–85 tour took him on the road around the world and back again to his own hometown where millions of fans showed up to hear him. The tour may be his last for a while. The Boss is not going to retire, but he's going to enjoy a well deserved rest.

No one does it like Springsteen! Ross Marino/Sygma

HAPPINESS AND FAME

While resting Bruce may take time to ponder or think about a new album. Or perhaps he may consider a movie role. Especially since his two good performances in the rock videos "I'm on Fire" and "Glory Days," both directed by John Sayles were so well received. Bruce is said to have a friendly relationship with the camera. Just as he does on the stage, he gives electrifying performances on the videos.

"I'm on Fire" is a short three minute video with a white T-bird car, a set of car keys, a girl's hand, and Bruce. And at the end of the video, "Glory Days," we see The Boss in a baseball hat, pitching to an imaginary San Diego team until he's called away by a beautiful blonde, who just happens to be Julianne, his wife.

Videos are very popular these days and

becoming very powerful. A good video can really help the sale of an album. And a bad video can work the other way.

"I wanted to be involved in videos in some way," Bruce says, "but there were problems involved. The song already tells a story. I didn't want to change it to fit a video." The audience's imagination had already formed pictures that he didn't want to change.

The same with making movies. When he writes a song, it tells a story in six minutes. To rewrite it to fit an hour and a half movie could really change the meaning.

For new writers, Bruce had a few words of caution. "You write about struggling along. Then you write about making it professionally. Then somebody's nice to you. You write about that. It's a beautiful day, you write about that. That's about twenty songs in all. Then you're out. You've got nothing to write."

Bruce writes when he's inspired. He doesn't write every day. Somedays he just relaxes.

One of the songs on the *Born in the USA* album was made into a single. "Dancing in the Dark" was given a dance beat like Cindi Lauper's, "Girls Just Want to Have Fun," and it's doing very well. There are other songs Bruce and the band have recorded but they didn't fit into anything. Maybe while the boss

Clarence Clemons playing a mean saxophone—Philadelphia 1985. Tom Herde

Bruce and his entire band take a bow—Giants Stadium, 1985. Robin Platzer/Images

is resting up from his tour, he'll go through these songs and put them together so we can all enjoy them.

Bruce admits he's not a planning type. When he's not working he likes to take life easy. Long drives in one of his cars and playing pool are pastimes he enjoys. But when he does work, he thinks deeply. And it shows in his lyrics. In thinking back over his career so far, he says he's learned a lot. Even the lawsuit experience and the lay off he had to endure taught him a valuable lesson: to relax and keep a focus on what is real and important.

Fortunately, he didn't suffer from the lay off at all and he now has over eight million fans.

The August 1985 edition of *Newsweek* magazine featured Bruce on its cover. A lot has certainly happened since 1975 when he was first featured in that magazine!

What keeps him going now that he's reached his dream and is on the high road? His own words sum it up nicely, "You gotta follow your dream and hope you're headed for higher ground." There's no doubt that for Bruce Springsteen, the sky's the limit!

DISCOGRAPHY

The records speak for themselves! Bruce Springsteen's rise to fame and the formation of the E Street Band in 1974 have given music lovers more than a decade of spectacular rock and roll. In addition to the albums and singles The Boss and the E Street Band released themselves, Bruce contributed many songs to other artists' recordings. The titles listed here are those released by Bruce Springsteen and the E Street Band.

ALBUMS (Columbia Records)

1973 GREETINGS FROM ASBURY PARK, NEW JERSEY

"Blinded by the Light"; "Growin' Up"; "Mary Queen of Arkansas"; "Does This Bus Stop at 82nd Street?"; "Lost in the Flood"; "The

Angel"; "For You"; "Spirit in the Night"; "It's Hard to Be a Saint in the City"

THE WILD, THE INNOCENT & THE E STREET SHUFFLE

"The E Street Shuffle"; "4th of July, Asbury Park (Sandy)"; "Kitty's Back"; "Wild Billy's Circus Story"; "Incident on 57th Street"; "Rosalita (Come Out Tonight)"; "New York City Serenade"

1975 BORN TO RUN
"Thunder Road"; "Tenth Avenue Freeze-Out"; "Night"; "Backstreets"; "Born to Run"; "She's the One"; "Meeting Across the River"; "Jungleland"

1978 DARKNESS ON THE EDGE OF TOWN
"Badlands"; "Adam Raised a Cain"; "Something in the Night"; "Candy's Room"; "Racing in the Street"; "The Promised Land"; "Factory"; "Streets of Fire"; "Prove It All Night"; "Darkness on the Edge of Town"

1980 THE RIVER
"The Ties That Bind"; "Sherry Darling"; "Jackson Cage"; "Two Hearts"; "Independence Day"; "Hungry Heart"; "Out in the Street"; "Crush On You"; "You Can Look (But You Better Not Touch"; "I Wanna Marry You"; "The River"; "Point Blank";

"Cadillac Ranch"; "I'm a Rocker"; "Fade Away"; "Stolen Car"; "Ramrod"; "The Price You Pay"; "Drive All Night"; "Wreck on the Highway"

1982   NEBRASKA

"Nebraska"; "Atlantic City"; "Mansion on the Hill"; "Johnny 99"; "Highway Patrolman"; "State Trooper"; "Used Cars"; "Open All Night"; "My Father's House"; "Reason to Believe"

1984   BORN IN THE USA

"Born in the USA"; "Cover Me"; "Darlington County"; " Working on the Highway"; "Downbound Train"; "I'm on Fire"; "No Surrender"; "Bobby Jean"; "I'm Goin' Down"; "Glory Days"; "Dancing in the Dark"; "My Hometown"

SINGLES   (Columbia Records)

1973   "Blinded by the Light" / "Angel"; "Spirit in the Night" / "For You"

1975   "Born to Run"/"Meeting Across the River"

1976   "Tenth Avenue Freeze-Out"/ "She's the One"

1978	"Prove It All Night"/"Factory"
1980	"Hungry Heart"/"Held Up Without a Gun"; "Jersey Girl"/"Cover Me"
1981	"Fade Away"/"Be True"; "Santa Claus is Coming to Town"
1982	"Atlantic City"/"The Big Payback"—released only in England
1984	"Dancing in the Dark"/"Pink Cadillac"; "I'm on Fire"/"Johnny Bye Bye"; "Glory Days"/"Stand On It"; "Born in the USA"/"Turn Out the Lights"
1985	"I'm Goin' Down"/"Janey, Don't You Lose Heart"